Self Employment

The Basics 2014

Faye Stevenson

Canterbury College

108472

Introduction

This book will help guide you along the way to starting up your own business or becoming self employed and give you the knowledge and resources you need to get your business off the ground, meet legal requirements, obtain funding, identify and appeal to customers.

The government have recognised that in order to get the economy moving we need people to become self-employed, especially if they have recently become unemployed or redundant. So now more than ever they are working on supporting individuals to start their own businesses as ultimately this will lead to more jobs. There are now loans and grants available along with business support schemes to help potential entrepreneurs take their first steps towards launching a successful business.

As you read the book you will become aware of the requirements to start a business, use it as a checklist to ensure you have all the boxes ticked, once you have completed it read back through the pages ensuring that you have every section of your business set up, your market awareness is up to date and you fully understand all the core elements of your business.

Directory

Why become self-employed?

There are many reasons why employment might not be right for someone, they may have been made redundant and have lost confidence in been taken on as they fear losing another job, they may have medical conditions that effect them working in the conventional sense, they could have family circumstances that make it hard to work around or they could have a specialist skill and are struggling to find companies locally that offers employment opportunities that are relevant. Due to this the government have made additional funding available to support start up businesses and growth and development of businesses already trading. Many of the government initiatives not only offer financial support but also the support of business mentors, who are typically successful entrepreneurs who have either retired or found themselves in a position to have free time which enables them to share the benefit of their experiences with new business owners. If you do a search on business support in your local area it will bring up details of your local delivery partners, most of these will offer free workshops supporting individuals to understand the basics of business and will cover the subjects mentioned in this book in more detail, they can also support you to put together a business plan and cash flow forecast for your business we'll talk about this more later.

Many people believe that they aren't able to become self employed as it is too much hard work and a complicated system. Self employment is a lot simpler than it looks. As long as you keep copies of all of your receipts and you make a copy of your invoices that you give to customers and each month you shouldn't have a problem. The key to running a good business is organisational skills. If you keep a good diary of where you have been working and when or what customers you have seen or what orders you have sent out you can't really go wrong. People tend to get in a mess when they forget about the administration side of the business and focus solely on the delivery of good and service, they then get to the end of the financial year and start to panic because they can't remember who they sold what and what suppliers they purchased off earlier in the year. As long as you keep your information in order and keep on top of your book keeping you will be fine.

One of the main attractions of becoming self-employed is that you will no longer have to work for somebody else there are several other good reasons to consider self employment this are:

- Flexible working hours
- Potential to work from home
- Self satisfaction
- Unlimited earning potential
- Flexibility for multiple projects
- Childcare – Able to work whilst children are at home

It's not all plane sailing being self employed, it takes commitment and you must have a general interest in the product that you are promoting or you will find it difficult to find the motivation to push your business forward. The disadvantages you should consider include:

- Not being certain of having a regular income
- Having to arrange your own sick pay, holiday pay and pension
- Having to work long hours
- Stress related to carrying the responsibility of making the business successful for yourself and your staff
- Can be difficult to focus on the business if working from home as family and day to day events can cause distractions.

You need to weigh the good up against the bad and think about your personal circumstances, can you afford to spend time building your business? How will you survive in the early days while you build your customer base? How much do you need to live on each month? This will help you to work out how much money your business needs to realistically make in order for it to be feasible.

What are you going to do?

If you are considering self-employment and do not already have an idea of what you want to do, you could consider something which uses your experience or skills or something which you have previously done as a hobby. Practically any job that you can do on an employed basis you can do on a self employed basis. Walk down to your local high street, look at the small family owned businesses that are operating in that area. Every single one of those businesses came about because someone woke up one day and decided I am going to start a business! Your business will take hard work and dedication and it will only succeed if you make it work, there are no quick wins business and it will take time to develop and grow. You need to look at your business not only as an investment in your future but your children's future. You have the opportunity to build something that can be passed on to future generations, you have the ability to build a business that will improve the lives of people in your community, it is a big responsibility but highly rewarding too. Some of the options available are:

- Gardener
- Child Minder
- Painter and Decorator
- Cake Maker
- Dog Walker
- Sales Person
- Hairdresser
- Driver
- Telesales
- Photographer
- Plumber
- Financial Advisor
- Computer technician
- Spray Tanner
- Book Keeper
- Online Marketing
- Personal Trainer
- Entertainer
- Personal Carer
- Mechanic
- Wheelie Bin Cleaner
- Jewellery Maker
- Mobile Sandwich Shop
- Teeth Whitener
- Personal Trainer
- Artist

You don't need to limit yourself to only one type of business, many people who are self employed make the most of several talents and the equipment they have available in order to use it to its maximum potential and supplement their income, for example a window cleaner might offer a gutter cleaning service or a patio washing service in order to generate additional income as they can utilise the same equipment. Some people have a multitude of talents; for example they could work as a freelance writer and submit articles on an ad hoc basis, but could also be a children's entertainer at the weekends and Monday to Friday operate a home telesales business. There is no limit to what you can do in order to help your business survive, the main thing is that you keep individual records for each area of the business to prevent yourself getting confused at the end of the tax year, also think about the advertising you do, how you market one aspect of your business might not be suitable to market another aspect, does each section of the business require its own website or are the services your offering interlinked enabling you have one website with sub categories. You also need to think about the cost related to this and if you can afford to have multiple websites.

If your business is complex and time consuming however you may find that you need to focus all of your energies on one area to get the business up and running, trying to do too much at once can leave you starting multiple projects but never really seeing a result. Focus on the main area(s) of the business and try and stick to it, set yourself targets in relation to different parts of the business and don't move on to the next one until the first one is complete. This will prevent you from getting carried away.

Training

Many professions don't require you to have completed a formal qualification in order for you to set your own business up, it is recommended as the qualification will give you the background knowledge of the area you are working in and it will reassure your customers that you know your stuff, however if you have been delivering your product or service for some time you can use customer testimonials and a portfolio showing examples of your work to give your customers piece of mind.

One common mistake that people often make is that they assume they are at the top of their game when in actual fact knowledge can quite quickly become out of date, especially in the environment that we now live were technology is expanding and changing to rapidly, there could be more efficient ways to deliver your service that you are not aware of. Also we live in the generation of red tape and healthy and safety, policies and procedures may have changed, do you require certain licenses to deliver your business, do the products you use meet today's Trading Standards expectations etc, completing a course relevant to your field of work will support you to gain this knowledge, The more you know about your industry the better the service you are able to offer will be.

Some professions will require you to complete training in order to register with their regulating body, for example a plumber offering gas services must be registered on the Gas Safe Register and in order to register they must have completed certain qualifications, this applies to child minders, financial advisors and various other sectors. It is worth looking into to see if your chosen profession requires you to register and who the regulating body is.

Training is available from a variety of sources such as:

- Local Colleges
- Community Venues
- Voluntary Sector Organisations
- Private training companies
- Universities

If you are claiming benefits some course fees may be waivered and if not you can look into Adult Learner Loans, these are available for courses costing over £300. You don't have to pay anything back until you're earning over £21,000 and repayments are minimal.

University has changed a lot over the years, they are now a lot more accessible than in the old days, before you would only be considered if you had completed three A Levels and they took two years to complete, now there are fast track courses called 'Access Courses' which allow you to progress to University within a year. Most universities offer part time courses and online study as well as full time courses to support people to be able to fit their studying around their current commitments whether it's a full time job, a business, family commitments etc. If you are looking at a university level qualification then you may be eligible for support with not only course fees but also a loan and grant to support you to live whilst you are studying, grants do not need to be paid back and most loans have a gap period before they require paying back in order to give you chance to focus on getting the job you actually want. Also you want pay anything back until you're earning over £21,000 and you will only pay 9% of the amount you earn above this. For more information on this go to https://www.gov.uk/student-finance

Legal Status

If you are considering self-employment, you will need to consider the different ways of trading and which would be the most appropriate for your business. The business could take one of three legal forms:-

- Sole trader. This is the simplest way of starting a business. Any money that goes into the bank is effectively yours, you are responsible for ensuring your creditors are paid as you will be liable to cover any business debts you incorporate and if you don't pay your creditors your home or any personal assets could be at risk. The plus side of this is if you have a good month and you want to take £2000 out for a holiday, then you can, you're not answerable to anyone but yourself.

- Partnership. This is similar to a sole trader except that two or more people run the business you are both jointly liable for any debts incurred through the business, it can be a good idea to ask a solicitor to develop a partnership agreement with a clear exit strategy which outlines how you will deal with affairs should the business cease to trade. This type of relationship works largely on trust as you will both have access to the business accounts, the safest way to run this is to make bank accounts require both signatures to release funds however this can be time consuming and may not be appropriate, you also need to ask yourself if you feel this is necessary and if it is why are you going into business with this person. Another issue that can occur is if one party has more personal assets than the other, if the business isn't successful does one person look to loose more than the other and if so you may want to look into a Limited Partnership.

- Limited company. This gives the business a completely separate identity from the people who run the business. It is more complicated to set up and you will probably require the help of a solicitor and an accountant. When setting up a business you decide the amount of money you wish to limit the company against, this can be as little as £1. If the business goes into administration your personal assets will not be taken into account, your business assets will be sold to raise collateral to pay back your debts but you will only be required to pay out of your own funds the amount you initially registered for. Being a limited company you do not have unlimited access to the companies funds, you will need to pay yourself a set wage as an employee of the company. In the beginning you may be required to take a reduced wage whilst the business gets up and running. As a director of the company you will e able to take dividends out of the business on a monthly, quarterly or annual basis. The advantage of dividends is that you only pay 10% tax. If you require more information on this then consult an accountant.

In addition to one of the above legal forms, self-employment can also involve one of the following trading practices:-

- a co-operative. This is a business which is collectively owned and controlled by the people who work in it. At least two people must be involved

- a franchise. A franchise is an agreement which allows the person buying the franchise the right to run a branch of a business that someone else has set up.

Registering your Business

Once you have decided what it is you are going to do you need to ensure you inform HMRC. You can now complete this online and it literally takes about ten minutes. Upon completing this you can decide whether you would like to apply for Small Earnings Exemption which means that you won't need to pay National Insurance Contributions if you are earning below £5885 per year. (There is more on this on page).

It is important that you inform the HMRC as soon as you start to trade, you can do this at any time throughout the year, and many people have the misconception that they need to register a business in April at the start of the tax year. This isn't true.

Once registered you will receive a Unique Trading Reference (UTR) this is similar to your National Insurance Number is will stay with you for the rest of your life, if you dip in and out of self employment you will still use the same UTR. If you are starting a partnership you will both receive individual UTR's.

This will come in the post and can take a couple of weeks to arrive however this does not prevent you from trading in the meantime. Once you have received this you will also start to receive monthly remittances for your National Insurance Contributions unless you have opted out. If you do not pay these you may incur a fine so you need to be organised, you can pay these at the post office or by direct debit.

The tax year typically runs from the first Monday in April, beyond this point you will be expected to start collecting information for the last tax year and you will have until the 31st of January the following year to submit your tax return, you can submit at any point, it is best not to leave it until the last minute in case there are any queries with your return. If you file your return late you will be charged £100 for every month that it is overdue, so it is very important that you keep on top of this.

Keeping Records

It is extremely important that you keep accurate and detailed records of the businesses income and expenditure. You may be able to keep your own books or you can employ a bookkeeper or an accountant, but if you are trading as a limited company you will most probably need the help of an accountant unless you have prior experience. An accountant can cost as little as £20 a month depending on what it is that you need them to do. The more work you can do yourself the more money you can save yourself, however I respect the fact that some things such as allowable expenses can be complicated and it is worth speaking to an accountant about this if you are unsure. Most colleges run basic manual and computerised book keeping courses, it might be worth looking into one of these if you have never had to do this before.

A simple accounting sheet for a hairdresser for one month can look like this:

Date	Income	Amount
01/04/14	Haircuts	£450
	Perms	£220
11/04/14	Extensions	£725
	Dye	£325
	Total	£1770
Date	**Expenditure**	**Amount**
01/04/14	Equipment	£350
	Fuel	£120
13/04/14	Phone	£40
	Chair Hire	£400
	Total	£910

Income – Expenditure = Profit

A the end of the month you list all of your sources of income and write alongside the amount that each one has generated, then you do the same for your expenses giving you two totals, deduct the total expenditure from the total income and the amount your left with is profit. You add up your profit for the full year and this is the amount you pay tax on. It's that simple. If the amount you have left is under the Tax Allowance for the year, you won't be due to pay any tax for that financial year.

The financial year typically runs from the 1st of April to the 31st of March and your Self Assessment is not due till the January following the end of the tax year. You can however start your financial year on a date that suits you better you will need to discuss this with the tax office.

Tax Allowance

As a self-employed person, you will be responsible for paying income tax on your earnings and will usually need the help of an accountant. There are special tax reliefs and allowances which self-employed people can claim. If you are newly self-employed, you should register with HM Revenue and Customs (HMRC) by calling the helpline for the Newly Self-Employed. The helpline number is: 08459 154515.

You can get more information about income tax for self-employed people from the HMRC website at: www.hmrc.gov.uk.

You can also use HMRC e-learning site, which explains all about tax, national insurance, self-assessment and other related issues when you start a business. Go to: www.hmrc.gov.uk

You can earn up to £10,000 a year(2014/2015) before you are required to pay tax, money received from benefits is classed as taxable income. (The amount will change every year, you can go to the Inland Revenue site to confirm the current Tax Allowance).

Registering with HMRC is simple it takes approximately fifteen minutes and can be completed online, you will need the following information to hand in order to register:

- Your National Insurance number. In most cases you'll already have this, but if you haven't worked in the United Kingdom before you'll need to get one.
- Your contact details (and the contact details of your business if you've started self-employment).
- Your ten-digit Unique Taxpayer Reference number, but only if you have previously completed a Self Assessment return. You'll find this on letters or forms sent by HMRC about your tax return.
- The date your circumstances changed.

To register go to www.hmrc.gov.uk

National Insurance

If you are self employed you are responsible for paying your own National Insurance. How much you pay depends on your profits:

Annual Profits	Class 2	Class 4
Up to £5,725	£0 but only if you get an exception	£0
£5,885-£7,956	£2.75	£0
£7,956-£41,865	£2.75	9% of profits from £7,956 up to £41,865
More than £41,865	£2.75	9% of profits from £7,956 up to £41,865 and 2% over that amount

You pay Class 2 either via direct debit once a month or every 6 months or you can ask HMRC to bill you twice a year. Your class 4 contributions will be paid with your Income Tax. You can set up your payments when you register for Self Assessment.

Value Added Tax

Value Added Tax (VAT) is a tax on goods and services which is paid to HM Revenue and Customs. Whether or not a self-employed person has to pay, and in some cases has the right to choose to pay, VAT depends on the type of business and how much the business sells. If your business has a turnover above £79,000 you will be required to pay VAT. Some goods and services are exempt from VAT, such as insurance and finance, education and training, and charitable fund-raising events.

If all of the goods and services you sell are exempt, your business is exempt and you won't be able to register for VAT. This means you won't be able to reclaim any VAT on your business purchases.

You can get more information about VAT from the website of HM Revenue and Customs at: www.hmrc.gov.uk.

Premises

You could consider trading in the following ways:-

- From home. This has the advantage of low costs but you will need to make sure that the tenancy agreement, mortgage agreement or title deeds of the property do not place any restrictions on business use. You may also need to get local authority planning permission if you need to make any modifications to the building. Depending on what business your running from home some require you to have a license such as beauty therapist and tattooist, you will need permission from the environmental health department and will need to ensure that you have correct agreements in place for things such as waste removal.

- From premises you have bought or rented. You should consider how much space you need as well as heating, lighting and ventilation requirements. You need to make sure the property has been approved for business use. Planning permission may also be necessary. If you are considering buying or renting premises you should see a solicitor. If you are looking at renting a room or a chair (for beauty type professions) you will need to think about if the business has the correct licenses in place to cover your type of business, do they have the necessary facilities in place or will you need to apply for planning permission and make adaption's to suit your business, you will need to check with the business person who's name the lease is in, the property owner and the local council if this is feasible.

- From a market stall. The local authority will have details of where and when these are available and how much local markets charge. You will need a market traders license and sufficient public liability, some companies won't cover market traders so you need to check this with them.

- At craft fairs. The local authority will be able to give details of where and when these are held or you can do a basic internet search, a good way of finding out about these locally can be to get in contact with your local Surestarts, voluntary groups, schools and see if you can have a stand at their events.

- From customers homes. If you have a mobile business and you go into the homes of customers, you will still need a base to register your business too, this will probably be your own home address however if there are restrictions on your tenancy it can be somewhere else where you have permission to operate from. You will need to consider when going into people's homes the insurances you need and if you require a DBS clearance.

When first starting out in business you need to consider if you can afford the cost of premises, this is the dream for most business owners however it can take time to build up to this and we all need to start somewhere. Having a physical address can add credibility to the business but it can also add additional unnecessary cost. Why not start selling your products at markets and then progress up to a shop? Or if you sell a service offer it on a mobile basis and once the demand for your service starts to grown you can then look taking on a space to do your administration work from or even store supplies.

Business rates

Business rates have to be paid to the local authority these apply to most business premises. These include shops, offices, warehouses and factories. In some cases, for example, in a property which contains a shop and a flat, or if you work from home, you may have to pay both business rates and council tax.

Some types of business premises are exempt from rates, for example, agricultural land. Depending what area you live in you may have temporary exemptions on Business Rates from the local council or reduced rates, especially in areas where they are trying to encourage enterprise. For more information about business rates in England, see the GOV.UK website or contact your local council.

Health and safety

As a self-employed person you have a duty to make sure that your business premises and working environment meet health and safety requirements. Further information about health and safety requirements is available from the local health and safety executive or environmental health department of the local authority.

Make sure that you have assessed the risks to:

- Your own health and safety at work
- The health and safety of other people you work with
- Your customers health and safety

Carrying out a risk assessment doesn't need to be complicated. Look around your work environment think about the potential hazards and ensure that you have a strategy in place for dealing with it if the worst was to happen.

If you have your own premises you will need to think about fire exits, toilet facilities, is there a first aider on site, where is the first aid kit kept, are the smoke alarms working, are there obstructions that could cause an accident should there be a fire. If you work from a building site think about the way you carry the building materials, any clothing you need to be visible and prevent injury, scaffolding and other equipment that needs to in place to ensure that materials are moved in an effective way to prevent injury.

If you drive a vehicle as part of your role how frequently is it serviced? If you work in people's homes, do you have a lone working policy, do you need a CRB? You need to think about every angle of your business, how do you keep you safe, your staff and your customers? Knowledge of your industry will support you to understand the risks associated with it and help you to develop strategies to prevent accidents from happening.

Do you need to do an induction for new employees/volunteers to ensure that they are aware of the sites health and safety policies and procedures and if so do you need to get them to sign to say that they have read an received this.

Insurance

Depending on the business and how you trade, you will be required by law to take out certain types of insurance. Other types of insurance are not compulsory but it is important to consider which ones are appropriate. The types of insurance you may need are:-

- employer's liability insurance. If you employ other people you must have this insurance. It provides cover for claims made by employees who are injured or become ill as a result of their employment
- vehicles insurance. Vehicles used for business purposes must be insured even if already insured for private use
- public liability insurance. This provides cover against claims by members of the public who have been injured or had property damaged as a result of carelessness at work by you or your employees
- premises insurance. Insurance will be necessary for the premises you work from, even if you work from home and there is already a policy. This is because the insurance will usually only cover residential use
- contents, stock and materials insurance. This insurance will be necessary to cover the replacement costs of stock, materials and the contents of the premises even if is work is being done from home and there is already a home contents insurance policy
- health and accident insurance. These will pay a regular income or lump sum if you are unable to work because of an accident or sickness.
- Indemnity Insurance

Pensions

As a self-employed person you will get state retirement pension if you have met the contribution conditions.

You could also consider getting a private personal pension. A personal pension will ensure that you are able to live to the standards that you have grown accustomed to throughout your working life. Pensions can work in several ways and it is best that you seek professional advice before deciding which on works best for you.

For more information you can go to the pension advisory service, they are a voluntary organisation who offer impartial advice on pensions, supporting you to get the package that's right for you.

For more details go to their website

http://www.pensionsadvisoryservice.org.uk/

Employing other people

If you employ other people you will be responsible for paying wages, tax and national insurance contributions where relevant. You will have to meet the requirements of employment law and health and safety regulations.

There are various schemes out there to support you to employ people if you are a small business

- Youth Wage Incentive Grant – offering employers up to £2275 per employee as long as the person you are employing meets the criteria for more information speak to your Local Jobcentre or Work Programme Provider
- Apprenticeships – Offering an Apprenticeship would give you the chance to support a person with their personal and career development and they can grow as your business grows. You will receive a £1500 grant to support you to employ the young person along with an assigned tutor and support with structuring the way the work based learning is implemented. You can contact your Local Job Centre or College for more information or go through a Private Training Provider.

Benefits and Tax Credits

Obviously when setting up in business the idea is that you will be so successful that you won't need to rely on state benefits, however it can be reassuring to know what you are entitled to when in the early stages of setting up. The most daunting prospect for people can be thinking about how you will survive whilst the business grows and although benefits should not be considered a long term option it is good to know that it my help as a stepping stone.

As a self-employed person you may be able to claim benefits or tax credits, depending on your income and other circumstances.

- If you are a lone parent you can claim working tax credits if you work above 16 hours per week.
- If you are part of a couple with children you can claim working tax credits if working over 24 hours
- If you have no dependants and are over 25 you can claim working tax credits if you work above 30 hours
- If you are over 25 and in receipt of ESA you can claim working tax credits if you work above 16 hours.

If you are in receipt of Disability Living Allowance you may still be eligible for this if you are self employed, it depends if your illness is affecting your mobility and the amount of care you require. You will need to explain how you are able to operate your business alongside your illness. There are support services in place to help people with disabilities to run their own business such as Access to Work. This scheme is put in place to enable people with disabilities to live a full life and have the same opportunities made available to them as everyone else. Access to work can support individuals with the following:

- Aids and equipment to support you in your work place
- Adapt equipment to make it easier to use
- Money for travel costs to and from work
- An interpreter if you have trouble communicating
- A support worker/job coach

If you want to find out more information about the Access To Work New Enterprise Allowance go to www.gov.uk/access-to-work

Trading names

You need to consider whether you wish to use your own name or a trading name for the business. If so, there are restrictions on the names businesses can use, certain words that are considered offensive are not allowed.

If you decide to go with a trading name, you need to consider two things, firstly is your business going to provide more than one service? If you are going to provide a window cleaning service but then also a web design service it wouldn't be appropriate to name the company 'Window Washers' as this only highlights part of your business. You can give separate parts of your business separate parts of your business separate names or you can trade under something generic like your initials so mine would be F.D.S. Also be careful not to come up with a name that is so confusing your customers can't find it or remember how to spell it, as they may not be able to look you up.

Another thing to consider is that your chosen name may already be being used; this isn't a problem as long as the other business is not a limited company or as long as they are not trading directly in your geographical area or to the same customer group, you don't want your customers accidentally finding their business when looking for you as this could result in a loss of sales. Also if you are planning on building a website, would you want it to have the same name as your business? If so it might be useful to look on a domain registration site like www.123-reg.co.uk to establish if your chosen name is available, if not you may be able to purchase a variant of your chosen name.

Licenses

You may need to get a license depending on the type of business, it is best to speak to someone within the licensing department of the Council to find out what these are as they can vary from district to district.

You can use the Governements License Finder tool to establish what licenses you might need to run your business and what the process is to apply.

Go to https://www.gov.uk/licence-finder for more information

Finance

As a self-employed person, you will need enough money to live on as well as money to start up the business and keep it going. You may be able to get money from the following sources:-

- Family or friends may be able to help you out depending how much it is you require and what their current circumstances are. It should not be assumed or taken for granted that they will help you out as your business is a risk for you so will be an even bigger risk for them.

- Grants from charities or trusts are available. A grant means that you will not have to pay the money back however you may be asked to provide evidence of what you have spent the money on

- Loans from banks and building societies will require monthly repayments they can typically be split over 1 and 5 years depending on the amount you borrow. The typical APR is around 16% but this can vary depending on your personal circumstances, if you have been with your bank a while you may get a preferential rate however if you have bad credit you may be expected to pay back your loan with a higher rate of interest to cover the provider against the risk of lending. Some loan providers will consider a break between being granted the loan and the first repayment being made.

- Credit Unions offer a savings and loan scheme where they will offer you a loan however the amount available will depend on how much you have in your Credit Union Savings Account, the interest rate is minimal and they are very user friendly, you can find out more information by going to http://www.findyourcreditunion.co.uk/

- You may need to take an employment opportunity whilst you start to build your business, you will need to take into account that the job must pay you sufficiently to cover your living expenses alongside allowing you to make savings to put towards your business.

Start up Funding

Princes Trust

If you are aged 18-30 and are currently unemployed you can access various schemes and grants.

Development Awards are available to support you with expenses that are not part of your business start up but that might support you to get to the point where you are able to start thinking about your business idea. They offer cash grants of up to £500 to help young people get into education, training or employment. These can cover the following:

- tools or equipment for a job or qualification e.g. hairdressing kit, carpentry tools, chef's whites

- course fees

- interview clothes

- license fees e.g. CSCS card (construction) or SIA license (security)

- childcare costs to help single parents access short term education

- transport to a new job until first pay cheque

The Princes Trust also run an Enterprise Programme, if your unemployed or work less than 16 hours per week you will be eligible to attend. This course is designed to make you look at self employment over the space of a four day course and to help you decide whether self employment is right for you.

The programme can give you:

- Training to give you a taste of what you need to know and do to start your own business

- One-to-one support to help you to explore and test your idea and turn it into a business plan

- Support to apply for a low interest loan of up to £4,000 for a sole trader and up to £5,000 for a partnership to help you to start your business*

- Mentoring to help you develop your business or access other opportunities in education, training, work or volunteering

To find out more go to http://www.princes-trust.org.uk/

Government Start-Up Loans

This is a government funded initiative which provides business start up loans and experienced mentors to people looking at running their own business. The maximum loan is £10,000 however the average loan is £5,700. There will be several providers within your region who have been allocated to distribute these loans. They can support you whatever level your business plan is at, whether it's a vague idea or you have a completed plan and cash flow forecast, they will make recommendations to help you move your business forward and support you through the application process.

To apply to start up loans and be allocated a business advisor within your region go to www.startuploans.co.uk

Finance Finder

The Government have launched a tool called the Finance Finder to help you establish what support is out there for your business, it's not a one stop shop so don't forget to look at other sources however it is still a handy tool to explore. If you are in the fortunate position to be eligible for a grant this means that you wont need to pay back the money given to you, however you will be faced with a set of restrictions on what the money can be spent on, you may be asked to provide evidence of expenditure and proof of the results you have achieved as a result of this funding. A loan works slightly different as you do need to pay the money back and although you will be asked to identify what you want the money for there is no monitoring process to ensure that it has been spent on what you say its going to be spent on with this in mind though you still need to ensure that the funds are spent in a way that will ensure your business can generate sufficient income to pay it back as your businesses future will be at risk. The finance finder will help you to establish what loans or grants are available to you and your business. To use this go to https://www.gov.uk/business-finance-support-finder

Local Councils

It may be worth contacting your local Council and speaking to the Regeneration Department as they may have small pots of community funding available as well as reduced business rates for start up business etc. This will vary from Council to Council. You can try your District Council and your County Council as they may have different support available.

Basics of Business Plan

If you are trying to get your business up and running or needing you are wanting to expand you will need to obtain funding. Whether it's a loan or grant that you are trying to access you will need to put together a business plan. A business plan helps give the funder the full pictures of what your business involves and how you plan to make money from it.

Most people panic at the thought of putting together a business plan as it can seem complicated and daunting, however if you have already researched the industry that you want to move into it should be a doddle.

There are a lot of free guidelines online to get you started so even though I am going to talk you through the basics of business planning you can look for a template that suits you. The amount of information required for your business plan will really depend on the scale of the project.

If you are a sole trader window cleaner looking for £500 funding to buy ladders, buckets and squeegees you wouldn't be expected to write a plan with the same level of detail as someone looking to invest £15,000 into a window cleaning franchise. You may ask the question as to why you would want to invest £15,000 into a franchise in appose to starting up for yourself and there are many reasons such as brand recognition, infrastructure, business support and national marketing campaigns. We will touch on this in more detail later but these are the types of things that a funder would want to know. If you were going to become a sole trader you could be competing with a large franchise so how can you compete with them? What is your unique selling point, how can you guarantee the service you offer your customers will be better.

Initially the first thing a potential funder will want to know is who you are, and any other partners in the business.

- What expertise do you bring to the business?

- Do you have any prior experience in this sector?

- Do you have any relevant qualifications?

- Do you have any links that would be beneficial to the business?

A business plan is pretty much putting into words all of the things you would have considered when making the decision to set your business up.

- What do my consumers want?

- When and where do they want it?

- Is it an essential item or a luxury item?

- How often would they need my service/product?

- How much would they be willing to pay for it?

By answering these questions you have a starting point for your business plan, by identifying the need for your product you can establish if your proposed business is feasible and if so you might then want to look at developing a full business plan. If your feedback doesn't show a need for your product you might decide to go back to the drawing board before progressing with your business plan.

To obtain the answers to these questions you need to ask people. This means going beyond your comfort zone, not only speaking to family and friends but speaking to unbiased members of the public. You need to ask a reasonable number or people in order for you to identify trends. Alongside asking the above questions you might want to ask the age and sex of the person, you may need to know what area they live in and what their buying habits are, are they homeowners or living with parents, are they in employment etc.

These types of questions can help you to understand who your target audience are. If you are selling patio furniture you might establish from your research that the people that said they would be likely to buy your product fall between the 29-59 age groups, mainly male, in employment and a home owner. This information would fit into the market research section of your business plan, it will show a potential funder that you understand what your customers want and that you know the audience that you are going to promote yourself to.

Effective marketing is the key to any business and if you know exactly who you are marketing your business to it can make life a whole lot easier.

There are several methods of marketing that can be effective and you need to decide which one is right for you, these include:

1. Local newspapers, depending on the size of your business and the type of service or product you are offering you may want to advertise in local newspapers, this can be costly though and your adverts are in competition with any other advertisers. A cheaper alternative is to look at parish and local community magazines who usually charge around ¼ of the price.

2. Networking, irrelevant of what your service is, networking and word of mouth is one of the best ways to let people know about what it is your offering. You are your own number one salesperson and the more people see you out and about, know your name and face, the more likely they are to think of your service. You can attend networking events either as a stall holder or just as a visitor, make sure you take business cards so that people know how to get in contact with you after the event.

3. Leafleting, this can be hard work for not a lot of return, make sure you are strategic when thinking about were to deliver your leaflets, if your company do children's parties, is it worthwhile taking them around an area that is predominantly bungalows, yes it may generate the odd referral from a grandparent or a family member, those leaflets could be better placed being delivered in an area with family housing. Think about the demographic of the area, are they typically working families in this area? Leave leaflets in shops, community centre's, Surestarts etc practically anywhere you can that way your leaflet can generate several leads instead of just one. There are companies that you can pay to deliver bulk loads of leaflets it might be worth looking into one of these as your time could be better spent doing something else.

4. Sign writing can be useful on cars, vans or even buildings, as once you have paid there are no ongoing advertising costs. However have a think about it how often have you stopped to read the back of a van, how many people actually pay attention to them? Think about the price of the sign and how many referrals you would need to generate in order to pay for itself. If the cost of the sign is £200 and it generates 4 sales over the period of a year for £150 each then have you really got anything to lose? If you look at sites like www.vistaprint.co.uk they offer great deals on magnetic signs for cars, you can get one from as little as £8, bargain!!

5. Promotions can help bring in sales, if you're a new business maybe you're going to offer an introductory offer or a discount on the customer's first purchase. You will still need to use one of the above mediums to advertise your promotion but it can be a great way of getting someone interested in your business. Whether its buy one get one free or a money off voucher, just remember you don't want your business to run at a loss so identify your profit margins before setting the offer so you can ensure you are covering the cost of the item/service.

6. Radio offers the ability to make your advert into something real. Customers can hear it, if it's catchy they can sing it, the most successful adverts can sometimes be the most annoying because the customer can't get it out of their head. The best example of this is a certain car insurance website, when you think of car insurance you can't help but sing the catchy tune and that's how they get their adverts to stick in our heads. Radio advertising can e expensive and you have to think about the sort of return you can expect to generate from this.

7. I have saved the biggest one till last, the internet. The internet is a marketers dream. There are so many avenues to explore it would be impossible to compress all the information into one paragraph so I have dedicated section three of this book to online marketing. Have a good read through and establish what type of marketing is right for you and your business. You may need to brush up your IT skills, there are a lot of courses available through local colleges

Once you have established how you are going to promote your business you need to think about how many sales you expect these avenues to generate. What return are you going to get on your investments?

When considering the amount of sales or bookings you expect to make you also need to consider how long it takes you to make your product or deliver your service, can you accommodate all the bookings you get? Your advertising campaign needs to be relative to the size of your business. A sole trader plumber working in Clapham would not benefit from posting a full page add in the Yellow Pages as it would be expensive and you may find yourself turning away work as people would assume you are a large national company with several plumbers on your books, on the other hand that money may be better spent having a full page advert in the local paper as this would cut down travel time and costs and provide a more realistic workload. Once you have placed your advert you will need to consider when the phone starts to ring how much are you going to charge your customers? The best way to do this is research what your competitors are charging and compare the service you offer to the service they offer. Is yours better value for money, or do you offer a quicker turn around etc. You can use this knowledge as a key selling point in your advertisements along with entering it into your business plan to help you gain the funding you require.

You might work out from this advert that you expect to get one big job and two small jobs per week; in monetary value this could like this:

1 big job = £500

1 small job = £40

1 big job + 2 small jobs = £580pw

To work out how much this would total on an average month you would multiply it by 52 and divide it by 12. So for the above it would be:

£580pw x 52 = £30,160

£30,160 / 12 = £2513.33

You can then transfer this information on to your cash flow forecast. If you are struggling to make sense of this you can ask a business advisor or an accountant to help you complete this.

The main thing is that you work out your income as above and you also work out your expenses for the business on a monthly basis, such as premises, insurance, advertising, stationary, utilities, travel costs, this will have to include the wage that you will pay yourself and ideally this will be enough to cover your living expenses.

It can be a good idea to write down your monthly outgoings, listing everything from housing costs, groceries, toiletries, travel, clothing, childcare etc. Whatever this figure comes to gives you the amount you need to incorporate into your cash flow as your monthly salary.

The total amount of your predicted income minus the total amount of your anticipated expenditure will leave you your profit for the year. If your business is running at a loss in the first year you may be expected to prepare three years worth of cash flow so the funder can see at what point you expect the business to be running at a profit and when they can expect a return on their investment. Don't forget to factor in the loan repayments into your business plan as this can be the key to you gaining approval.

As stated before your business plan can contain as much or as little information as you want it to, however the more comprehensive the plan is the more chance you have of gaining the funding you require. No one is going to give you money without being sure that you fully understand the business sector that you are going into. The more research you can do about your industry, your customers and your competitors the more chance you have at being successful.

Once you have started your business you can refer back to your business plan to see if things panned out the way you expected them to, once you get in the momentum of running your business and servicing your customers it can be easy to forget about things like monitoring your competition, comparing suppliers prices and your marketing strategy, so use your business plan as a guide and a reminder to review this things.

How to generate online sales

Over 36 million British people use the internet everyday; that's more than 50% of the population, it is being accessed by a laptop, mobile , TV, games consoles etc. The internet has become the world's fastest growing form of communication and the most effective marketing tool for businesses.

Building a Website

The first place to start when looking at online marketing and generating online sales is a personal website. You should ideally pick a domain name to list your business under that is related to what you're doing to help people search it.

If your business is called Scotty's Electro Designs and a potential customer wanted to find you, unless they were already aware of your business and know to search your business name, they might not find you, Electro is an abbreviation of Electronics and it might not be a term what customers would think to search under. If website was called www.electronicdesignsuk.com it would have more chance of being found on Google.

You can build a free website using the websites listed below:

www.webs.com

www.wix.com

www.moonfruit.com

www.yola.com

www.sites.google.com

There are many more sites out there and it's really down to personal preference, some are easier to navigate round than other. Most of these sites of a basic package for free but I would recommend upgrading to a package that gives you a personalised domain name as sub domains do not list on Google searches. These sites will enable you to build the site to meet your needs, whether you just need a basic info page with contact details on and examples of your work or you need an e-commerce site that has facilities to take payments.

When writing the content for your site ensure that you use words that are relevant to the products you are selling, perhaps have a blog page which explains how to use your products or testimonials page so people can discuss their views on it. The more relevant words that describe your product/service, the more searchable your site will be on Google. However be careful not to overuse key words and ensure you incorporate them into full sentences otherwise this will flag your site up as spam to Google and they will remove your listings.

Below is a table outlining the benefits and disadvantages to making your own website;

Promoting Your Website

This is the next issue, its all well and good having a site but if no one knows it's there what's the point in it? In order to generate hits to your site you need to do the following to:

1. Submit your website to search engines, not sure how to do this, its simple. Go to Google and type in 'submit my website to search engines'. Most pages will submit your site to multiple search engines saving you time, you literally just type in your domain name.
2. Utilise free adverting, the likes of: www.Yell.com www.freedirectory.com www.vivastreet.com www.gumtree.com www.freeads.com Having listings on these sites and linking your website to them will help pull your website up on Google listings as it will be a more recognised site, this is called creating back links. These sites also provide you with traffic as people can directly click through from those sites on to your website.
3. Make the most of social networking, we will cover this in more detail later but social networking sites can help you target family, friends and people living in your local are by the power of people sharing and liking your posts, make sure you put your website link on it.
4. Google Adds and Pay Per Click campaigns can be costly but useful to target people of a certain demographic. You can set your own budget and decide what search terms you want to be searchable under. Be cautious that some companies invest hundreds of thousands into this type of marketing and if you put a very generic term in like Electronics, your £100 budget isn't going to get far compared to their £100,000 budget, plus you could get enquiries from people all over the country, is your business prepared to deal with that type of demand. However if you use Electronics Southwell as a keyword, you're more likely to come up as its unlikely the big companies will be using key words targeted to small villages and you will attract customers from your local area.

Pros	Cons
Flexibility to edit the content of site when you want	Must have a reasonable level of IT Skills
Low start up costs	Time consuming
Able to add and remove products at your own discretion	The package may be limited and not provide features that you require
Some sites come with free Google adds vouchers	No ongoing support
Able to monitor unique hits through site control panel	

Ebay

You can either link Ebay to your own personal website or solely trade using an Ebay shop eliminating the need to have a website, it really depends on what sort of impression you want to give your customers. Having a professional looking website nowadays can be as credible as having an actual shop. Back in the dark ages when the internet had just launched and no one trusted online services and banking and everyone was scared of being conned having a website didn't fill people with much faith, now virtually the whole world is online and a companies credibility is now questioned if they don't have a website. However it depends on the types of products you are selling and the volume you plan to sell. If you are buying a broken TV's, repairing them and selling them on and you can only manage to do 2 or 3 a week for people living in your local area, you may not need a full website. If you are able to do 20 a week on a regional basis and are offering money back guarantees, warranties etc. You might want a website to link to your Ebay which shows all of your Terms and Conditions, Testimonials, contact details etc. Before selling your products on a marketplace, you'll want to make sure you have a good sense of your margins and a firm understanding of the marketplace's fee structure, if your product has a low profit margin the fees might not be justifiable.

Pros	Cons
Customers search through listings so you don't need to pay advertising costs	Have to pay a percentage of the final selling price to Ebay along with listing fees
Benefit from worldwide marketing	Need to be IT literate
You can add a widget to your site that shows your active Ebay listings	Time consuming
Promotions such as 'no listing fees days'	Customers can leave bad feedback
Be rewarded for good customer service with positive feedback	Have to pay Paypal fees on top of Ebay fees

Amazon

Amazon searches the net to find listings of the products you're looking for to save you time. Alongside this you can also sell on Amazon using the Amazon Market Place. Unlike Ebay Amazon is not an auction site, the prices are fixed. They offer set fees, if you are a small business you can list your items for £0.75 and if you are a power seller your account will cost you £25 a month however you will still pay a percentage of your final sale price back to Amazon. They are currently promoting no fees for 3 months if you sign up for a power seller account.

Payments cannot be made until you have been registered for 14 days and take between 3-5 days to reach your bank account.

By listing your items on Amazon you can reach millions of potential customer's every day, not only can customers buy your goods, they can create Amazon wish lists in order to enable family members and friends to know what they want for birthday and Christmas presents.

Alongside this you can use Amazon fulfilment. You sell it, they ship it. Amazon has created one of the most advanced Fulfilment networks in the world. With Fulfilment by Amazon (FBA) you store your products in Amazon's Fulfilment centres, and they directly pick, pack and deliver them as well as provide customer service. You can even offer your products for sale on other Amazon Marketplaces in Europe (Germany, France, Italy and Spain) and they fulfil these orders from your inventory stored in the UK.

Amazon also offer a Pay per Click advertising service to help your generate more response from your listing, alongside your items been seen in general listings they will be shown on adverts on the bottom and sides of the pages when people are searching related items.

Pros	Cons
International sales potential to millions of worldwide users	Slow payment turn around
Low insertion fees	Final seller fees can be costly
Utilise Amazon Inventory for storage and delivery	Shopping fees are set at fixed rates
Multi advertising strategy including, Pay Per Click, wishlists, generic listings.	Customers are owned by Amazon not you; you cannot contact customers who have previously purchased from you.

Gumtree

Depending what your business is offering there are various ways of using Gumtree to promote your business. You can list items you have for sale in the 'For Sale' section. You can post adverts for free however the main issue with this is that adverts go on in date order of posting so after a day or two your listing will no longer show on the first page, to keep you listing showing on the top of the front page you can pay a fee to have it listed as a featured add. Depending on what your selling this can vary from £3.75 up to £35, you pay more to be featured on the front page of the website.

If you are promoting a service you can either post in the services section or the community section depending what it your advertising. You can promote anything from plumbing, hairdressing to singing lessons here. It is free to post however you are faced with the same problem that after a few days you will lose your front page listing due to the adverts being posted in date order. To have a featured ad in this section costs £24.99. This may seem expensive however it depends how much the service is that you're advertising.

If your business is a multi level marketing business, such as Herbalife, Avon, Kleeneze, the most effective way of marketing your business is to post a job in the job section. You are given 5 free adverts and there after they cost £17.50 each, you will be required to pay additional fees to make your ad a featured advert.

Pros	Cons
Well known online presence, large volume of hits	Adverts are moved to the
Low insertion fees if you are selling a high priced product/service	Limited to number of free adverts you can place
Sellers can contact you direct and make own payment arrangements	Not moderation, no feedback on sellers so bad buyers who pull out of sales aren't highlighted
Easy to use	Listings aren't automatically removed when your item is sold so you can continue to get enquiries

Multi Level Marketing Schemes

Avon, Kleeneze, Betterware, Herbalife, operate by getting you to sell their products however alongside this they want you to build a team under you to sell the products. You not only make a commission on your sales but also their sales, if they go on to be team leaders and recruit a team you make money on their staffs sales as well and so on. You can purchase a Herbalife website for £8 per month which has all the products listed and enables your customers to buy products directly from the site, the order and payment is sent to you, you then log on to the main website and make the same order with a 25% discount. You keep the difference. Most of these companies work in a similar way and you can use the likes of Gumtree, Facebook, Twitter to build your team.

Pros	Cons
Well known companies can support you to build your team	Some bad press due to people not understanding how the scheme works and not being successful
Large support groups on Facebook to get advice and guidance	Customer needs to be highly motivated to make it work
Profit margins are clearly identified	Some companies require initial outlay for products, catalogues, brochures etc and require you to have minimum orders before you can become a team leader
Easy to use	No secure payment method.

Drop Shipping

These sites work similar to the Herbalife site. You pay a monthly fee for your website which covers hosting and basic maintenance. You then look through the Drop shipping pages and decide which products you would like to list. This can be anything from, clothing, make up, TV's, household products etc. You upload the products you want to sell and set the price you want to sell them at ensuring you have a sufficient profit margin to justify the sale. The order then goes through to you and the payment is made to your bank account. You purchase the same item from the wholesaler and send them a payment of the price they have listed the item at. You get to keep the difference and the item is sent directly to the customer. This is great because you never actually hold any stock so you don't have high overheads, you can run a fully functional shop distributing large items all over the world without ever leaving your own home.

There are various sites you can use that offer you the full package of buying a website, domain name, and supplying the products, however you can build your own site and place the products on that too. A few examples of good drop shipping sites are

http://www.dropshiptraders.com/

http://www.dropshiponline.co.uk/

www.shopify.com/free-trial

www.wholesaledeals.co.uk

www.brandsdistribution.com/**Dropshipping**

Pros	Cons
No upfront money for stock required customer pays for everything up front	Need to be motivated as you will need to generate your own site traffic
Websites are easy to build	Upfront fees to join drop shipping sites
Wide range of products available	Issues with deliveries are out of your control
No need to deal with shipping and returns	Must be generally IT literate

Online affiliation sites (Groupon/Wowcher/BuyaGift/Just Eat)

These sites work by targeting companies who have a product or service to offer, some are geographically targeted others are national. They sell a product for a reduced promotional rate and take a commission for each unit they sell. This can be used to sell anything from holidays, food, beauty services, car repairs, training sessions etc. The idea is that they make consumers aware of businesses and products they wouldn't usually be aware of and the company makes money from the repeat service. There are two things to consider when promoting yourself on these types of site:

1. Can you meet the demand? If your product is being promoted on a national scale do you have the ability to offer your service nationally? If you're based in London and you get a sale in Glasgow how would you cope with this? Selling products isn't too bad as you can post the item and specify additional postage charges however if you are only currently set up to demand with local sales and you are selling handmade photo frames and all of a sudden your product is on sale nationally on a well known website and you pull in 1000 sales over night can you deal with the demand? You don't want to take orders then let people down because you hadn't planned to expand that quickly, before considering this you should make a full business plan to ensure you have thought it through.

2. Are you going to make a profit? How much of a deduction do you offer, some of these sites specify that you need to offer at least a 30% or more discount from the original price, plus you need to take into account their commission. Can you afford to sell your products at this rate, how can you be sure that the customers generated from this site are going to be return customers? You don't want to sell your services at cost and end up with no customers and no profit. You need to make deductions that still offer you a profit margin and if you can't then don't sign up.

Pros	Cons
Benefit from national marketing campaign which generates traffic	Need to be able to deal with high volume orders (are resources available? staff, materials etc)
Raise awareness of your product/service, sell to customers who weren't aware of you	Difficult to sell products/services for profit
Target geographical areas or sell nationally	Need to be able to service large areas in appose to small villages/towns
Generate Bulk orders	If a customer buys a voucher for your service and doesn't redeem the voucher the site benefits and not you

Etsy/Folksey

Websites like this provide an affordable platform to sell your arts and craft items from. Working very similar to Ebay however they are not auction sites, people list handmade items for a set price. The benefit of having a shop on one of these sites in appose to launching your own site is the traffic they generate. They take the leg work out of finding customers as they generate the traffic you just need to make your items stand out above the other items listed on the site, whether that's by the price, the quality or the uniqueness of your item.

Facebook

You can start a page on Facebook for business purposes. Many people use the albums section to post pictures of their products giving it a description which explains the product and the price. Followers can use the message section to enquire about the product and to arrange orders and delivery. This is a free service. The best thing about selling on Facebook is that you can build a large audience quite quickly. If your friends and family share your items , like or comment on them this alerts their friends who in turn can do the same and the information is shared with their friends and quite quickly your page can go from local to international. Alongside this you can promote your page or the posts on your page which outline specific products by using the Facebook targeted advertising feature.

Tendering sites

(Myhammer, babysitter, eaupair, people per hour, five squids, MyVan)

These types of sites put the consumer in charge, by being able to post a job that they would like carrying out, they either state a price they would like the job done for or give you the option to put a quote in for the job and then pick the one they feel meets their needs. The problem with these sites is that a consumer cannot see the quality of the product that is on offer therefore a hardworking joiner who pays attention to detail and ensures the customer is happy before a job is complete could lose out to a shoddy worker who is good at talking the talk via email. One way to ensure that your work is showcased is to post profile pictures that show off your work, post links on your profile to your personal website were more examples can be find and if possible include testimonials or references.

Skype/VoIP Cheap

There are various businesses that can be run via Skype/VoIP cheap etc. These can include

- ➢ Technical support lines
- ➢ Advice and Guidance such as counselling
- ➢ Call Centres, sales

You would still need to link your business to a payment system such as PayPal and might need a website to promote your business; however it is a great way to keep the overheads down. If you plan to have an outgoing call centre it is not essential for you to have a website as there are companies that you can purchase specific data from. If you Google 'Purchase Debt data' you will find companies offering you the ability to purchase lists of peoples details who have recently applied to debt management companies, for debt consolidation loans or bankruptcy and IVA orders. You simply ring through the data identifying anyone who is interested in a debt management plan and sell that persons details on to a company dealing with the service you have promised the customer. You don't need an online presence as you are acting as an agent for the company you are selling the leads on to and you are going to the customers not waiting for them to come to you, you just need to ensure that you meet all of their terms and conditions and have policies in place for data protection and confidentiality. It sounds simple and it really is.

Mass Mailers (MailChimp/Squirrelmail/Turbo Mailer etc.)

If you have your own website you can add sections onto this were people interested in your site can subscribe in order to keep up to date on your latest products and new. Some sites require you to register and as part of their terms and conditions you are agreeing to receive promotional emails from them. You can use sites like Mail Chimp, Mass Mailer, Squirrel mail etc to compile a mailing list. This will allow you to add in the email addresses of your customers and send out a generic email in one go. Building the initial list can be tedious however some of the free websites mentioned earlier will automatically add customers who subscribe to your mailing list to save you even more time. You can send one email and target 1000's of customers in one go.

Paypal

Most of the methods of selling above require a way for businesses to be able to receive payments, of course you can give out your bank details but this isn't the most secure way of working and also can be hard to monitor who has paid what into your account. Receiving payments via Paypal gives you the details of the purchase, what site it has come from, what the item is, how much it cost, the date the order was made and gives you the ability to print a receipt off. You can withdraw money from Paypal into your business account. PayPal charges sellers a fee of between 1.4% and 3.4% on the total sale amount plus a fixed fee of 20p per transaction. The fee depends on how much you sell so the more you sell, the less you pay. PayPal is free whenever you use it to buy something or make a payment in the UK. As a buyer, we will not charge you to use PayPal unless it involves currency conversion.

As you can see there are many different ways to promote your business online, you need to think about what plays to your strengths and weaknesses and what is the best approach for your business and meets your available budget. Don't think you need to do all of the above select the few that you really want to focus on, once you have mastered them maybe look to explore other paths and don't forget the internet is changing all the time, people can lose interest in a website over night, new sites with fancier apps and services become available making sites seem less attractive. You need to keep up with the times and find out what the current trends are.

Summary

You should now have a basic knowledge of business terms and requirements, marketing and online promotion along with putting together a business plan and obtaining funding to get your business up and running. The more you learn about your business, the area you want to trade in, your competitors and your customers the more successful you will become.

Don't forget your business plan is an evolving document and even when you are established and up and running it is a good idea to review your business plan, your marketing techniques, research your customers needs and collect feedback in order to improve the quality of the service you are delivering. Technology is being updated all the time, if you review your business annually you may find quicker, cheaper, more effective ways of delivering your service or creating your product. Trends may change and this could result in an increase/decrease of sales.

Your online presence can mean the difference between becoming a flourishing business and going out of business. Task yourself with getting to grips with Social Media and using it to promote your business; the internet is your friend and the most effective, free marketing tool that you have access to so use it to your advantage!

The final most important thing is to make sure that you have informed the tax man and if you are claiming benefits the Job Centre! The HMRC are not out to get you, to avoid falling into trouble make sure that you are open and transparent about what you are doing. Remember the old saying 'honesty is the best policy'. Well it's true!

So long as you do everything listed in this book then you should have no comebacks on your business! If you get stuck and need more support then please see the list of Business Start Up Services in the back of this book.

Who can give further advice?

Banks

The services offered by banks vary greatly and so do the fees they charge. Some banks have special teams who handle business accounts. They may also have useful information for start-up businesses. It's a good idea to shop around for business banking services, for example, by using a financial comparison website.

The British Bankers Association has a website that can help you find the business account that suits you. For more information, go to: www.bba.org.uk.

Chambers of Commerce

A Chamber of Commerce is a local network of businesses. It can provide information, advice and training to businesses in your area. Most give free advice to members, but charge for services to non-members. Some Chambers of Commerce serve particular ethnic minorities.

GOV.UK

GOV.UK has information on setting up and running a business on its website at www.gov.uk.

Local enterprise agencies (England, Wales and Northern Ireland only)

Local enterprise agencies give free general advice and support to small businesses. Training courses are also available, which are often free. Details of local enterprise agencies are available from the National Federation of Enterprise Agencies - see below.

Citzens Advice Bureau

The registered office of national Citizens Advice is:

Citizens Advice
Myddelton House,
115-123 Pentonville Road,
London, N1 9LZ

This is an administrative office and no advice is available here.

Follow the link to find your local office
http://www.citizensadvice.org.uk/index/getadvice.htm

National Federation of Enterprise Agencies (England and Wales only)

12 Stephenson Court
Fraser Road
Priory Business Park
Bedford
MK44 3WH
Tel: 01234 831 623
Fax: 01234 831 625
E-mail: enquiries@nfea.com
Website (general): www.nfea.com

NFEA is a network of local enterprise agencies in England and Wales. Its general website has details of how to find you're nearest local enterprise agency.

Local authority economic development units

Some local council have set up units which give advice and help to businesses in their area. Some have bilingual advisers and are intended particularly to help ethnic minority small businesses. They tend to be mainly in inner-city areas. The advisers are employed by the council and will usually have a business background or related skill, such as banking or accountancy.

Women In Business Network

WIBN
The Grange
East End
Furneux Pelham
Nr Buntingford
Herts
SG9 0JT

If you have a general enquiry contact website@wibn.co.uk

National Federation of Small Businesses

England and Wales

Sir Frank Whittle Way
Blackpool Business Park
Blackpool
Lancs.
FY4 2FE
Tel: 01253 336 000
Fax: 01253 348 046
Website: www.fsb.org.uk

British Franchise Association

85f Milton Park
Abingdon
OX14 4RY

Tel: 01235 820470
E-mail: Contact form available at www.thebfa.org
Website: www.thebfa.org

The British Franchise Association (BFA) is the trade association for franchising companies. It was set up to promote franchising and establish standards. To join, franchising companies have to show that their franchise works and they have to agree to abide by a code of ethics designed to protect franchisees.

The BFA produces an information pack (£29 including postage and packing) for prospective franchisees which includes a list of checks to be made before buying a franchise.

The Prince's Trust

England

Prince's Trust
9 Eldon Street
London
EC2M 7LS

Tel: 020 7543 1234
Freephone helpline: 0800 842 842
Minicom: 020 7543 1374
Fax: 020 7543 1200
Email: webinfops@princes-trust.org.uk
Website: www.princes-trust.org.uk

The Princes Trust run programmes that encourage young people to take responsibility for themselves – helping them build the life they choose rather than the one they've ended up with:

PRIME Business Club

PRIME is a national charity dedicated to helping older people (over 50) start and run their own businesses. PRIME stands for the Prince's Initiative for Mature Enterprise. If you are thinking of becoming self-employed, it will provide you with a free start-up pack and provide information about local organisations that can help. It can be contacted via its website at www.primebusinessclub.com.

LiveWIRE

England and Wales

Livewire
Hawthorn House
Forth Banks
Newcastle-upon-Tyne
NE1 5JG
Tel: 0191 261 5584
Fax: 0191 261 1910
Website: www.shell-livewire.org

The Shell LiveWIRE programme offers free online business support and start up awards of £1,000 and £10,000 funding to young entrepreneurs in the UK (England, Scotland, Wales and Northern Ireland).

Acas (Advisory, Conciliation and Arbitration Service) (England, Wales and Scotland only)

If you are an employer, you can get free advice on employment matters from the Acas website at www.acas.org.uk and on its telephone helpline, 0845 747 4747. Acas also provides training courses on employment topics that may be useful for small businesses. The Acas Equality Direct helpline, on 0845 600 3444, provides a confidential advice service on discrimination and equalities issues.

Federation of Small Businesses

Head Office
Customer Services 0808 20 20 888

Federation of Small Businesses
Sir Frank Whittle Way
Blackpool
Lancashire
FY4 2FE

The Federation of Small Businesses aims to to be and remain the largest and most effective organisation promoting and protecting the interests of the self employed and small business owners within the UK.

Disabled Entrepreneurs Network (England and Scotland only)

Website: www.disabled-entrepreneurs.net The Disabled Entrepreneurs Network is a regional networking service for disabled people. It provides advice and support for disabled people who run their own business or who want to set up in business.

Notes